What Are the Summer Olympics?

by Gail Herman

illustrated by Stephen Marchesi

Penguin Workshop

For Lizzie—gymnast, sprinter, and more—GH

PENGUIN WORKSHOP
An Imprint of Penguin Random House LLC, New York

Visit us online at www.penguinrandomhouse.com.

Library of Congress Control Number: 2016935024

ISBN 9780448488349

10

Contents

Opening Ceremony, 2012 Summer Olympics

What Are the Summer Olympics?

Every four years during the summer, athletes from every corner of the globe meet to compete in the Olympics—the greatest sports contest on earth.

For about two weeks, athletes test their skill, their strength, and their luck in more than three hundred events. Arenas for the Olympics become a world stage, with billions of fans following the Games on TV.

There have been generals, princes, and movie stars who have competed in the Olympics. But more often than not, athletes are ordinary young men and women. Except, of course, they are not ordinary. They are champions in running, jumping, swimming, rowing, cycling, gymnastics, tennis, and soccer. Name any warm-weather sport, and most likely it's been played at the Summer Olympics.

Weeks before the athletes meet, the Olympics have actually already begun.

Where?

In Olympia, Greece, the site of the original, ancient Olympic Games. There, in a valley surrounded by gentle hills, a mirror is held up to the sun. The rays light the flame on a torch.

The Olympic torch will be carried to the city hosting the Games. The journey connects the Games of today to the Games of the ancient past. Long ago, fires burned in front of temples to honor Greek gods. Today the torch is passed from person to person moving by foot, car, train, boat, plane, through countries, across oceans, over mountains. On the way to Beijing, China, in 2008, the torch even reached the highest point in the world, Mount Everest.

But no matter its path, the relay ends at the Olympic stadium of the host city in time for the opening ceremony. The last torchbearer lights a cauldron, a giant bowl sitting atop the stadium. And the Games begin.

CHAPTER 1
The Ancient Games:
776 BC–AD 393

The Olympic Games started in Greece in the valley of Olympia at least three thousand years ago. Much about them is unknown. But one thing is certain. At first, they were part of religious festivals. The festivals were held to honor Zeus, the king of the gods worshipped by ancient Greeks.

The first known Olympics took place in 776 BC, but they may have started hundreds of years earlier. These early Olympics took place on a single day. There was a 200-meter race, among other events.

Why this length? Supposedly that was the distance the famous Greek hero Heracles (Hercules) could run while holding his breath.

In time, a stadium was built. More races were added. In one, athletes ran in full armor. Mostly though, they didn't wear anything at all. They ran naked!

Soon chariot races were added, as well as wrestling and boxing matches—which sometimes ended in a fighter's death.

Before each Olympics, messengers traveled through Greece, spreading news of the Games and seeking male athletes. No women could compete.

For each Olympics, thousands made their way to Olympia. Hundreds of tents lined the valley.

Campfire smoke filled the air. Magicians and fortune-tellers performed. Art and music exhibitions were held.

But as centuries passed, people stopped believing in the Greek gods. They lost interest in the Games. By AD 400, after more than a thousand years, the Olympic era was over.

CHAPTER 2
The Modern Games Begin:
The Late 1800s

In the 1870s, archeologists came to Olympia to learn more about ancient Greece and the Olympics.

Archeologists dig up buried objects to find out about the past. The archeologists in Olympia found bits of old vases and statues. These objects provided clues about the Greek way of life and its focus on having a strong mind in a strong body.

News of their findings spread. Many people already knew about the ancient Olympics. But the dig spurred renewed interest in the Games.

A teacher from France named Pierre de Coubertin was fascinated by this mind-body connection. He thought sports contests could help young people become better students. His goal was to hold Olympic Games again, with athletes from all over the world competing.

In 1894, Coubertin met with representatives from many countries in Paris, France. They decided the Olympics

Pierre de Coubertin

would be held every four years, each time in a different country. The first would take place in Athens, Greece, not far from Olympia. Two years later—about fifteen hundred years after the last Olympics—the modern Games began. That March, the US team of fourteen men sailed for Greece. There were no events for women at all.

It took more than two weeks by ship and train for the Americans to arrive in Athens. They joined more than two hundred athletes from thirteen countries— England, France, and Germany among them. To welcome the athletes, there was a special banquet, a parade, and dancing and singing in the streets.

Early the next morning, crowds flocked to the stadium, which was built from ancient ruins. It connected the new to the old. The Games began like the ancient ones, with a sprint.

The marathon—a long-distance footrace—was the final track event. The Greeks hadn't won a race yet. They wanted this win badly. Seventeen runners stood at the starting line in the city of Marathon. At 2:00 p.m. the starting gun fired. A French runner sprinted into the lead. The roads were hot and dusty. Doctors followed in carts.

At the halfway mark, the French runner held a long lead. But then the course went uphill. The runner slowed down and finally stopped.

An Australian took the lead. A bicyclist was sent ahead to announce his win. But one Greek runner, Spyridon Louis, was gaining ground. He closed the gap.

"Hellene! Hellene!" shouted Greek fans, meaning "A Greek! A Greek!" Louis ran even harder. The Australian fell to the ground.

Finally, Louis entered the stadium. A band followed on horseback. The king and queen of Greece and seventy thousand others cheered as he crossed the finish line first. Did he go on to further fame?

No!

Legend has it, Spyridon Louis never ran again.

The Marathon

According to legend, a Greek soldier fought in a battle in the town of Marathon. After racing twenty-five miles to Athens to announce the victory, he collapsed and died.

At the first modern Olympics, the longest race followed the ancient soldier's route. A few years later, the race was extended; today a full marathon is always 26.2 miles.

Swimming events took place next. There was no Olympic pool. The men headed out to sea. Hollow pumpkins floated in the chilly, choppy water to mark the finish line. The water was so cold that, at the 100-meter race, one American supposedly jumped in, shouted, "I'm freezing!" then climbed right back into the boat.

For the 1,200-meter race (almost three quarters of a mile), swimmers swam to shore from boats.

Many swimmers struggled. Some gave up.

The winner, Hungarian Alfréd Hajós, finished in 18 minutes, 22.2 seconds, just happy to be alive.

Founder Pierre de Coubertin was pleased with the Games. He was sure the Olympics would only get better after this. Instead, they almost fell apart.

CHAPTER 3
The Olympics Grow:
The Early 1900s

The next two Olympics were held in Paris and in St. Louis, Missouri, as part of world's fairs. World's fairs show off new products and inventions from different countries. In St. Louis, for example, many people tried foods like cotton candy and peanut butter for the first time.

But hardly anyone knew about the Games. The Olympics, which included women now, were a failure.

1904 World's Fair
in St. Louis

Women in the Olympics

Women first competed in 1900, in tennis and golf, plus a few other events. American golfer Margaret Abbott was the first to win gold in an all-female contest—competing against her mother! By 2012, with the first women's boxing contests, female athletes were competing in every sport. Now they make up about half of all competitors.

Margaret Abbott

From here on, Olympic officials decided the Games should stand alone. It was a wise move. After the London Games in 1908, Olympic buzz grew. And in 1912, at the Games in Stockholm, Sweden, an athlete from the United States became the first true Olympic star.

Jim Thorpe, who was part Native American, was born in Oklahoma Territory in 1888. At seventeen, he was sent to school in Pennsylvania. Glenn "Pop" Warner, the football legend, was one of Jim Thorpe's coaches. At a track meet, someone asked Pop Warner where his team was. All he did was point to Thorpe.

Jim Thorpe

At six feet tall and 190 pounds, twenty-four-year-old Thorpe came to the Olympics to compete in the pentathlon. That was a five-event contest including the long jump, javelin and discus throws, and two running races. People said that Thorpe barely practiced. It didn't matter. He won every event except the javelin. Then he went on to a ten-event contest called the decathlon. He won that, too.

The king of Sweden congratulated Thorpe, saying, "Sir, you are the greatest athlete in the world." According to Thorpe, he answered, "Thanks, King."

It's a great story—except for its sad ending. A year later Thorpe's medals were taken away, because he'd been paid for playing minor league baseball. It wasn't a lot of money. Still, getting paid at all made Thorpe a professional athlete. And only amateurs—unpaid athletes—were allowed in the Olympics.

Thorpe tried to explain. He wrote a letter to officials, saying he didn't know he was doing anything wrong. And he wasn't trying to hide anything. The officials didn't budge.

But thirty years after Thorpe's 1953 death, the Olympic Committee had a change of heart. His medals were returned to his daughter in 1983, and his name was put back in the record book where it belonged.

Olympic Medals

Today, first-place winners receive gold medals, second place get silver, and third place, bronze. But while athletes received medals at the very first modern Olympics, only the top two finishers were honored. They were given silver and bronze medals. There were no third-place winners, and no gold medals yet.

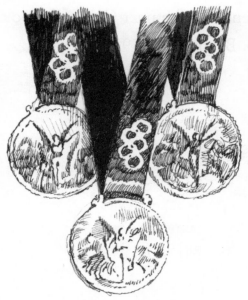

CHAPTER 4
New Games, New Stars: The 1920s

Because of World War I—which broke out in Europe in 1914—there were no Games in 1916. But in 1918 the war ended. The next Olympics took place in Antwerp, Belgium, in 1920.

Duke Kahanamoku

Americans starred in the water. Hawaiian Duke Kahanamoku, known as "the Father of Surfing," who had won two gold medals in the 1912 Olympics, again came in first in two swimming races. And fourteen-year-old New Yorker Aileen Riggin competed in diving.

Back then, women weren't allowed to dive in public indoor pools. So Riggin had to travel an hour to get to a beach. She had to time it right, too. She needed to be there at high tide. Other times, the water was too low.

In Antwerp, swimmers and divers competed in a moat that circled the city. The bottom was so muddy, Riggin feared she'd get stuck when she dove.

For her last dive, she dove off a tower, went into a slow somersault, then slipped feetfirst into the water. She became the youngest gold medal winner yet—and the smallest! She stood just four feet seven inches tall and weighed sixty-five pounds.

In the 1920s long-distance runners from Finland, "the Flying Finns," were also gaining fame. Paavo Nurmi was the fastest of all.

Nurmi won three gold medals and a silver in 1920. Then, in the 1924 Paris Games, Nurmi was

Aileen Riggin

entered in both the 1,500-meter race (not quite a mile) and the 5,000-meter race (a little over three miles). The finals were only an hour apart. How could anybody run both races?

But Nurmi was strong. And he carried a stopwatch to keep him on pace.

Nurmi checked the watch throughout his first race. He tossed it aside near the end, speeding up

Paavo Nurmi

for the final kick. He crossed the line way ahead of everyone else. What did he do next? Without stopping, he picked up his watch, then headed to the locker room to get ready for the next race.

An hour later, Nurmi won the 5,000. He left Paris with five gold medals.

US swimmer Johnny Weissmuller—from Chicago—was also the talk of Paris. He was only twenty years old. But he wasn't nervous in the least. While other swimmers got into position for a race, he was chatting and laughing with . . . a group of women.

"Come on, Weissmuller," one official said. "Only five seconds to the start."

"I'll be there on time," Weissmuller replied. "Don't worry."

He won the 100-meter race (two lengths of the pool) in 58.6 seconds, a world record. He won two more medals that day, *and* wowed crowds with a funny diving act.

Weissmuller would win two more gold medals in the next Olympics before he retired from competitive swimming. But fans could still watch him. He played Tarzan of the Jungle in twelve popular movies.

Johnny Weissmuller

In May 1928, Amsterdam in the Netherlands hosted the Summer Olympics. The Games were growing. Now, more than three thousand athletes competed in more than a hundred events, including horseback riding, sailing, tennis, and fencing.

At the opening ceremony, the Greek team led the Parade of Nations for the first time. It became a custom that continues to this day.

For the first time, women ran in track events. Sixteen-year-old Betty Robinson from Chicago had only been in three track meets before the Olympics. One afternoon, she was running from school to catch a train. A teacher saw her. He was so impressed, he had her practice with the boys.

Now Robinson was at the Olympics, running the 100-meter event. She was so nervous, she brought two left shoes. She managed to find a right one. And she won the race in world-record time: 12.2 seconds.

Robinson became the first woman to take home track gold.

Three years later, she was in a plane crash. Thought to be dead, she was brought to a funeral home. It turned out that Robinson was alive but in a coma. It took years for her to recover. But in 1936, she was back in the Olympics, part of a gold-winning relay team.

Betty Robinson

CHAPTER 5
Politics Enter the Games: The 1930s

The United States hosted the Games for the second time in 1932, during the Great Depression. All over the world, people had lost jobs and homes. Many countries couldn't afford to send athletes. So the host city of Los Angeles built the first Olympic Village. It had dorms for male athletes, a hospital, post office, and more. Female athletes stayed in a luxury hotel nearby. Famous Hollywood movie stars, including Charlie Chaplin, attended the Games, bringing excitement and glamour.

Charlie Chaplin

One athlete, Mildred Didrikson, didn't care about the celebrities. Her goal was simple: to be the greatest athlete ever. She was from a large Texas family, and had always played sports with boys. She could hit home runs like Yankee legend Babe Ruth. So everyone called her "Babe."

At twenty-one, Didrikson was not afraid to speak her mind. She didn't like wearing uncomfortable stockings for the opening ceremony. "[A]s for the shoes, they were really hurting my feet," she later wrote.

Nothing hurt Babe's performance.

She won the javelin throw. In hurdle events, athletes leap over a series of standing frames, almost like bars, as they run. Babe won the 80-meter hurdles race—and broke a world record. In the high jump, she won a silver medal, and thought she deserved gold.

In later life, Babe became a pro golfer, winning eighty-two tournaments.

Babe Didrikson

Adolf Hitler

Berlin, Germany, was chosen in 1931 to host the 1936 Games. In 1933, the Nazis came into power. Their leader, Adolf Hitler, wanted all of Germany to be Aryan, a term he used to describe a "pure" white race, a race that didn't include Jews and other minorities. He passed laws that took away these minorities' rights and freedoms.

Hitler saw the Olympics as a way to show the world that Aryan athletes were the best. The only German Jewish athlete allowed to compete was

Men's 1936 German Olympic Gymnastic Team

a half-Jewish fencer. Hitler thought this could convince the world that everything was okay. That his government was not anti-Jewish.

Even so, some US groups didn't want an American team to be part of the Summer Games in Germany. But the US Olympic Committee felt the Games were awarded to a city, not a government. The decision was to attend.

Some Jewish athletes chose not to go. Some went and couldn't compete, most likely because of their religion.

Meanwhile, in Berlin, signs saying No Jews ALLOWED were taken down from stores and restaurants. This was done to cover up what was happening in Germany. Olympic banners were raised, along with Nazi flags.

At the opening ceremony, more than a hundred thousand people filed into the brand-new stadium. Hitler arrived to huge cheers.

One of the first events was the high jump. In the high jump, athletes jump over a crossbar sometimes set more than seven feet off the ground.

Did Aryan Germans win? No! Two black Americans, Cornelius Johnson and Dave Albritton, took gold and silver, and a third American took bronze. Hitler left the stadium before their medal ceremony. It was reported that Hitler said,

Gold-medal winner
Cornelius Johnson

"Do you really think that I will allow myself to be photographed shaking hands with a Negro?"

Over time, the story changed into Hitler snubbing one American in particular: the most successful athlete at the 1936 Olympics, Jesse Owens.

Jesse Owens
(September 12, 1913–March 31, 1980)

James Cleveland Owens, born in Alabama, was one of eleven children. Everyone called him J. C. until a teacher asked Owens his name and thought he said, "Jesse." The new name stuck. Owens went on to be a track star in high school and college, where he was not allowed to live in a college dorm because of his color. Even after his amazing performance at the Olympics, he could only find odd jobs to support his family, including running in "stunt" races against horses and cars. Eventually Owens found success speaking about his experiences. In 1976, he received the Presidential Medal of Freedom, one of the highest honors in the United States, from President Gerald Ford.

Owens won three gold medals in track. But his long-jump win meant the most. The long jump is a jump for greatest distance. Owens was hoping to jump at least 26 feet. He already held the world record at 26 feet, 8½ inches.

But in a qualifying round, when Owens took a practice run into the pit—not even jumping—officials counted it as his first try. He was rattled. According to Owens, that's when the German jumper Luz Long came over. It turned out that not all Germans believed in Hitler.

Long gave him a tip for the jump. Owens listened. And he went on to win gold.

Long rushed to congratulate him. The black American and the blond, blue-eyed German became friends. Owens said that was more important than any of his medals.

Luz Long with
Jesse Owens

Friendship—and teamwork—helped the US rowing team, too. In the 1930s, rowing was a popular sport. Races were front-page news. There were even trading cards of rowing athletes, who were known as oarsmen.

At the Berlin Olympics, the American team was made up of friends from the University of Washington in Seattle. They were sons of poor farmers and fishermen and lumberjacks.

The oarsmen bonded while training. An eight-man rowing team works like a machine with eight moving parts. A ninth man, the coxswain, sets the pace, telling the others how fast or slow to row.

On the day of the race, a cold rain fell on the lake. The United States was in lane six, the farthest from shore—and the least protected from harsh winds.

The flag dropped to start the race. While other boats surged forward, the US team stayed in place. They hadn't seen the signal!

Even with the late start and the wind and rain, even with a sick oarsman, they slowly gained on the other boats. After pulling up to the first boats, the Italian team and German team, the American rowers gave one last stroke and crossed the finish line. Had they won?

Yes! By less than a second! In an amazing upset, these boys from Seattle took home gold. They remained friends for life.

Ancient Greek pottery depicts an Olympic athlete

Athletes race on this ancient Greek urn

The opening ceremony of the first modern
Olympic Games in Athens, Greece

Archers face off in the 1908 Olympics in London

Jim Thorpe (USA) throws a discus at the 1912 Stockholm Olympics

Mildred "Babe" Didrikson (USA) practices her javelin toss for
the 1932 Los Angeles Olympics

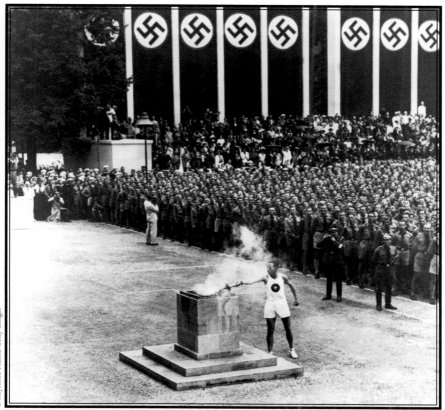

The cauldron is lit at the 1936 Berlin Olympic Games

Olympic swimmer (USA) Johnny Weissmuller

Jesse Owens (USA) and Ralph Metcalfe (USA)
compete in the 400-meter relay in Berlin

Tommie Smith (USA) and John Carlos (USA) raise their fists in a
black-power salute at the 1968 Olympic Games in Mexico City

Six of the eleven Israeli Olympic wrestling team members killed during the 1972 Munich massacre are photographed, from top left to bottom right: Moshe Weinberg, Yossef Romano, Mark Slavin, David Berger, Ze'ev Friedman, and Eliezer Halfin

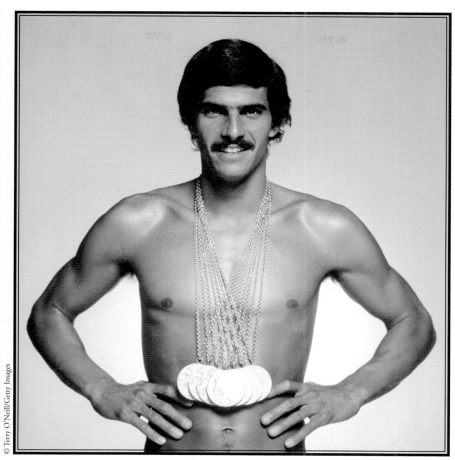

Swimmer Mark Spitz (USA) wins seven gold medals at the
1972 Summer Olympics in Munich, Germany

Track-and-field star Carl Lewis (USA) competes in the long jump during the 1984 Olympics in Los Angeles

Greg Louganis (USA) mid-dive at the 1988 Olympics in Seoul, South Korea

Gold-medal gymnast Kerri Strug (USA) is carried to
the podium on a sprained ankle in 1996 at Atlanta

Stephen Kiprotich (Uganda) leads the pack in the men's marathon
at the London Olympics in 2012

Gold-medal gymnast Gabrielle Douglas (USA) performs
on the uneven bars at the 2012 London Olympics

Fireworks explode over the closing ceremony
at the 2012 Olympic Games in London

CHAPTER 6
After the War:
Late 1940s and 1950s

Hitler invaded Poland in 1939, sparking another world war. World War II didn't end until 1945. So the Olympic Games were canceled in 1940 and 1944. Many athletes had reached their peak during those years. They were past their primes by 1948, when London hosted the next Games.

Nazi troops

But the long wait did not stop Dutch runner and long-jumper Fanny Blankers-Koen. She had competed in Berlin. The best part, she said, had been getting Jesse Owens's autograph. By 1948 she was thirty, married with two children and pregnant with her third!

Fanny Blankers-Koen

Blankers-Koen, however, was determined to outdo herself in the London Olympics, and she did—winning all four of her races.

In this new post–World War II world, politics could no longer stay out of the Olympics. Israel was created in 1948 as a homeland for Jewish people. Germany was split into East and West. And in summer 1952, the Soviet Union—a gigantic country made up of Russia and other nations—sent its first team to the Olympics.

SOVIET UNION

EAST GERMANY

WEST GERMANY

ISRAEL

Cold War

The Soviet Union and the United States had fought together in World War II. But now the Soviet Union and the United States opposed each other in a "Cold War." There were no direct battles. It was more of a power struggle. The Soviet Union had one party, the Communist Party. The government had total control, owning all businesses and giving citizens little freedom. The United States, a democracy, had open elections and private enterprise (businesses owned by individuals, not the government).

One way to succeed in the Cold War was to win in the Olympics. Until the Soviet Union collapsed in 1992, there was heated rivalry between the two nations every four years at the Summer Games.

At Helsinki, Finland, in 1952, the United States won boxing matches, a basketball championship against the Soviets, and fourteen gold medals in track and field. But in other years, the Soviets led, especially in gymnastics and wrestling.

Just before the 1956 Olympics, the Soviet Union sent troops into Hungary to make sure the country stayed Communist. Weeks later, in Melbourne,

Australia, the Hungarian Olympic team came up against the Soviets in a water polo match.

Water polo is a ballgame with goals that is played in a pool. It can get rough, and this game was—right from the start. The referee suspended player after player from both teams. At one point, a Hungarian took a blow to the face. Blood poured from above his right eye.

The referee stopped the game, with Hungary ahead 4–0. The score would stand. Hungary went on to win the gold medal in water polo.

The "blood in the water" game made headlines around the world. Would these Games be remembered for violence and hatred?

No.

An Australian student named John Wing wrote to the Olympic Committee. He suggested that all athletes march as one team during the closing ceremony.

Athletes from all the different countries did walk together. They talked. They laughed. Briefly, the joy of sports overcame political conflict. And the march became another Olympic tradition.

CHAPTER 7
Time for Change:
The 1960s

By the 1960s, students and young people around the world were protesting for changes in government and equal rights for minorities.

In 1968, Mexican students even protested against hosting the Olympics, feeling it took government money away from programs for the poor. But in the United States, the focus was on race.

In 1936, gold-medal winner Jesse Owens came home to a country divided by race. By 1960, little had changed. The South was still segregated—black Americans had to live apart from whites. They couldn't buy houses in the same neighborhoods, eat in the same restaurants, or even use the same drinking fountains.

The 1960 Rome Games were the first to be shown on television all around the world. Some black Olympians felt the Games now offered an opportunity to speak up for equality. For civil rights.

Meanwhile, one African American was so busy speaking up, it seemed as if he were running for mayor of the Olympics. In fact, Cassius Clay talked mostly about himself. He bragged he would win a gold medal in boxing.

No one believed him. He was only eighteen. And he was facing the three-time European champion. But Clay was right. He took home gold!

Cassius Clay
(later became Muhammad Ali)

Clay Becomes Ali

Cassius Clay never took off his Olympic medal. But then, legend has it, he stopped at a whites-only restaurant in his hometown of Louisville, Kentucky. A gang chased him and tried to grab his medal. Disgusted by the hatred, Clay threw it into the Ohio River. When he became Muslim, he changed his name to Muhammad Ali. He took a stand for religious freedom and civil rights, and against war. Years later, he received a replacement gold medal, along with the United States Presidential Medal of Freedom in 2005 and the National Constitution Center's Liberty Medal in 2012.

In Rome, Ali was not the only African American athlete in the spotlight. The runner Wilma Rudolph was quiet, nothing like Ali. But what a champion she was!

Rudolph was the twentieth of twenty-two children, and grew up in Tennessee. As a very young child, she suffered from polio, a disease that left her barely able to walk. Rudolph was so sick, she hardly got out of bed for years.

Her family didn't have much money. But her brothers and sisters massaged her legs every day. Her mother drove every week to a distant hospital for treatments. By age six, wearing a brace, Wilma could walk. By eleven, she was playing basketball.

In Rome, Wilma Rudolph won two gold medals in sprints, the short-distance races. She won another gold in a relay—an event where four teammates take turns racing, each passing a baton to the next runner.

Wilma Rudolph

No one could believe Rudolph's grace or her speed.
"Don't blink," people warned, "or you'll miss her."

When she came home to Clarksville, Tennessee,
Rudolph refused to go to any segregated celebrations.

So her town held a parade in her honor with both blacks and whites marching together. It was the first time that had ever happened.

Two Olympics later, African American college students Tommie Smith and John Carlos wanted to make a difference for their race.

In the 1968 Mexico City Games, they were favorites in the 200-meter sprint, one half-lap around the track. In the final, Carlos took the early lead. Close to the finish, he turned to look for Smith. In that instant, Smith pulled ahead and took gold. Carlos ended up with the bronze.

At the medals podium, Smith and Carlos bowed their heads during the national anthem. Then they raised their fists in a salute that was a sign of black strength and unity.

Both wore civil rights buttons.

The Australian silver-medal winner wore a button, too. "I'll stand with you," he told Smith and Carlos.

For just saluting, Smith and Carlos were thrown off the US team. Back home, the two men received death threats. But Smith had no regrets. "We had to be seen because we couldn't be heard," he said years later.

Tommie Smith

John Carlos

Amazing Jumps of 1968

Everyone knows how to jump, but not everyone gets to do it at the Olympics! Bob Beamon did. Because their measuring device wasn't long enough, officials had trouble measuring his long jump. Finally, the result was announced: 29 feet, 2½ inches, almost two feet longer than the world record. Beamon, from New York City, never jumped that far again, and held the record until 1991.

Before this Olympics, high-jump athletes jumped upright, in a standing position. But Dick Fosbury, from Seattle, twisted his body, going over headfirst with his back to the bar. He took gold with 7 feet, 4¼ inches, and changed the sport forever. Now every high-jumper does the "Fosbury Flop."

Dick Fosbury

CHAPTER 8
Munich and Montreal:
The 1970s

In summer 1972, Germany was the host country for the first time since the 1936 Berlin Games. Officials planned for a calm, peaceful Olympics.

Instead, tragedy struck.

On September 5, eight armed men snuck into the Olympic Village. They were part of Black September, a violent Palestinian Arab group bent on getting rid of the country of Israel.

The terrorists forced their way into one building

housing Israeli athletes. Some escaped; two were killed right away, and nine athletes and coaches were held hostage, most from the wrestling team.

The Games were stopped. No one knew if they would go on. And everyone felt afraid. Meanwhile, the terrorists demanded a flight out of Germany. They wanted to take the hostages to Egypt. The German government agreed, but it had a plan to stop them.

It didn't work.

At the airport, a German police officer fired at the terrorists. Right away the terrorists returned fire. One tossed a grenade. All the hostages died, along with five terrorists and one German policeman.

The next day at the Olympics, a service was held for the Israeli victims. The Olympic president declared, "The Games must go on." The Israeli government agreed. Some athletes didn't feel that was right, and they left. "You give a party," one

Dutch runner said, "and someone is killed. You don't continue the party. I'm going home."

But others agreed that stopping the Games would be knuckling under to terrorism. Despite the controversy, the Games did go on. But of course it was not the same.

Before the attack, California swimmer Mark Spitz had dazzled crowds, winning all seven of his events—a record, at the time, and all in world-record times.

Mark Spitz

On the morning of the attack, he was ready for a news conference about his races. "I completely freaked out," Spitz, who is Jewish, said decades later. He feared for his own life. That very day, armed guards whisked him out of Germany.

Before the Munich attack, athletes had worried about performing badly. Losing. Now, after the tragedy, athletes knew it was possible to lose much more. Even your life. Still, they kept training, kept working toward their Olympic dreams.

Four years later, the Games were in Montreal, Canada. By then, gymnastics had grown hugely popular. Female gymnasts from Soviet countries

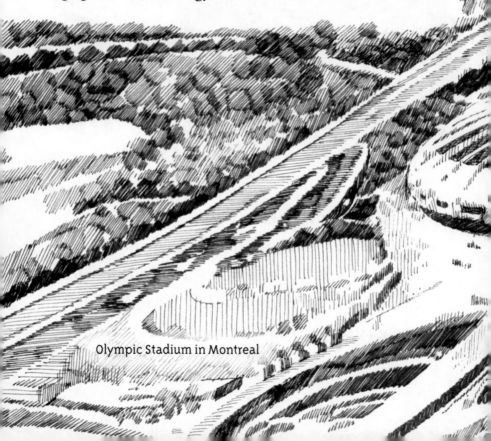

Olympic Stadium in Montreal

were capturing fans' hearts. One, Olga Korbut, had soared to fame in Munich even without winning the gold for the all-around.

Olympic Gymnastics

There are three parts to the competition. In the team event, athletes compete as a group on all the equipment. In the all-around, an individual contest, each gymnast is tested in all the events. In the second individual competition, each gymnast is judged in one event.

Men's Apparatus

Parallel bars: gymnasts swing between or above two bars.

Horizontal bar: gymnasts swing around one bar, performing handstands, twists, and other acrobatic moves.

Floor exercise: gymnasts do a tumbling routine on a mat.

Rings: gymnasts grip rings, holding themselves upright as they perform handstands and flips.

Pommel horse: gymnasts keep their bodies above the "horse" and swing their legs around its handles.

Vault: gymnasts jump over "the table" with a handspring, followed by flips and twists, landing on both feet.

Women's Apparatus

Women gymnasts do a floor exercise and perform on the vault.

They also use:

Uneven bars: gymnasts flip, twist, and swing, moving between a lower and higher bar.

Balance beam: gymnasts perform a routine moving along a long piece of wood, doing cartwheels, somersaults, and more.

Now in Montreal, at the 1976 Olympics, Korbut was Soviet captain. Would she lead her team to gold? Yes!

Would she capture the all-around title now? No!

Nadia Comaneci from Romania won gold.

At fourteen, Comaneci was the youngest gymnast to win the medal, and the first to receive a perfect score on the uneven bars. In fact, the judges gave her seven perfect scores!

Nadia Comaneci

Comaneci came home a hero. But life was harsh in Communist Romania. In 1989, Comaneci escaped. It was not easy; at one point she had to walk six hours through wintry countryside to sneak across a border. Eventually, she married American gymnast Bart Conner, and settled in Norman, Oklahoma.

Who Wins?

For some events, like gymnastics and diving, athletes are judged on a number scale—the higher the number, the better. The score takes into account both the difficulty of a stunt and how well it is performed. In many other Olympic contests, like swimming and running races, the first to finish wins.

Some races are very close. So how do officials know for sure who wins? Technology! In some cases, high-speed cameras show the outcome. In the pool, there are touch pads. Swimmers touch the pad when they reach the wall, sending a signal to a computer. In the shortest sprints, a laser beam is projected across the finish line. As runners cross, the beam is blocked, and a signal is sent to a timing device. It's all so different from the first modern Olympics, when officials used a plain old stopwatch.

CHAPTER 9
Dives and Drugs:
The 1980s

The 1980 Games were to be held in Moscow, the Soviet capital. Thousands of US athletes had been training for years in hopes of making it to the Olympics.

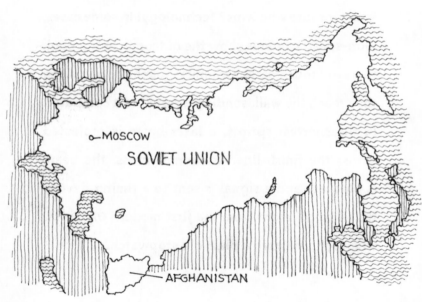

But seven months before the Games began, the Soviet Union invaded the country of Afghanistan. In protest, US president Jimmy Carter announced a boycott. No athletes from the United States would go to the Moscow Olympics. The Games weren't even shown on US TV. To this day, people still debate whether pulling out of the Games was the right thing to do.

How Do Olympic Athletes Make the Team?

Many countries have programs for outstanding athletes who want to become Olympians. Other athletes join sports clubs, or train on their own with a coach. Then they compete in regional contests. If they do well, they go on to state, then national competitions. If they win those events, or have top times in races, they go on to Olympic trials. Top performers make the Olympic team. There aren't any general age requirements. But certain sports have rules. Nowadays, gymnasts and weightlifters must be at least sixteen. Find out more at Olympic.org, the official website of the Olympics.

Olympic Stadium in Los Angeles

In 1984, Los Angeles was hosting again. Now the Soviets, along with thirteen other Communist countries, decided to boycott the Olympics. Most believe it was done as payback for Moscow.

The absent Soviet countries had dominated gymnastics since the end of World War II. Would anyone step up now?

Mary Lou Retton

Yes! A sixteen-year-old girl from a small mining town in West Virginia!

Mary Lou Retton had never competed in a big worldwide meet before. Now, in the all-around event, the top prize depended on Retton's

last performance on the vault. She flew off the springboard into a double-twist-back somersault. A ten! A perfect score! Retton was the first American—man or woman—to win gymnastics gold!

Like gymnastics, diving is another event that puts intense focus on a single athlete. Divers stand alone with millions watching as they perform incredible moves off the board.

In 1988, Seoul, South Korea, hosted the Games. And Greg Louganis was considered the best diver in the world. He had won a silver medal in the 1976 Games, and two gold medals in the 1984 Games.

At the 1988 Olympics, Louganis had to get through three rounds of diving. Each round required five or six different dives. Each dive is scored on its difficulty and how well it is executed.

Greg Louganis

Diving Events

In springboard diving, the diving board is on a coil, or spring, so it bounces as the diver jumps. In platform diving, athletes jump from a platform that doesn't move.

There are forward-facing dives and backward-facing ones. Somersaults and twists are performed in the "tuck" position (holding the knees tightly against the chest), the "pike" position (bending at the waist, keeping the legs straight), or the "free" position (the body vertical, twisting horizontally).

To get a high score, Louganis had to perform more and more difficult dives at every level, and perform them almost perfectly. Could he do it?

Growing up in California, Louganis had a hard time in school. He was teased for having dark skin. He had trouble learning to read. He turned to smoking and drinking before he discovered diving and found a place where he could succeed.

Now, at the springboard, Louganis was taking his ninth dive, a reverse two-and-a-half somersault, a very difficult dive. Louganis bounced on the diving board and leaped up. What happened was exactly what all divers fear. Coming down, he struck the back of his head on the board. He fell into the water.

Louganis managed to climb out of the pool. But he was bleeding. He was given stitches right then and there.

Half an hour later, he was back in action. And the next day, he nailed eleven dives, including

that same reverse somersault. Louganis won gold.
Then he won gold in platform diving, too.

Louganis sobbed when he realized he'd won.
But it was not from happiness. Six years later, he
told the world he was gay, and he explained his
state of mind at the Olympics.

Months before the Games, Louganis learned
he had the virus that could lead to AIDS, a life-
threatening disease. He was afraid he'd gotten

blood in the pool when he'd hit his head. He was afraid he had spread the virus. He was even afraid he might have passed it to the doctor who stitched his wound closed.

Today, we know AIDS is not that simple to catch. But back then, it was a different story. AIDS was hushed up. Many gay men had the disease. Wrongheaded people even thought it was a punishment for being gay.

Louganis was brave to get back on the diving board after his accident. But his announcement about his personal life took even more courage.

Greg Louganis ruled the pool for two straight Olympics, in 1984 and 1988. Carl Lewis hoped to rule track those same years.

Frederick Carlton Lewis grew up in New Jersey. Both his parents were track coaches. It seemed natural for him to run. He turned out to be so fast, the Dallas Cowboys wanted him on their team, even though he didn't play football.

Carl Lewis

Lewis stuck with track, training in the same events as Jesse Owens, his hero. In 1984, Lewis won four gold medals in sprints and the long jump.

In 1988, his first event was the 100-meter dash. The race has been called the greatest in history. It's also come to be called the dirtiest. Why? Many of the runners had taken drugs to improve their speed.

But at the start of the final, no one knew that. They only knew the fastest men on earth were running: Carl Lewis and Canadian Ben Johnson.

Johnson, in lane six, was the last to get into position. Lewis, in lane three, thought of his father, who had recently died. How Carl wanted to make him proud.

The gun fired. Johnson leaped into the lead. Lewis edged forward, ahead of the others. But he couldn't catch Johnson. Johnson crossed the finish line in an unbelievable 9.79 seconds. Lewis won silver. His time, 9.92, equaled the old world record.

A few days later, however, blood tests showed Johnson had taken drugs. He lost his medal for "doping." "From Hero to Zero" read one Canadian headline.

Ben Johnson's career was over, while Carl Lewis became an even bigger star. Lewis got the gold medal in that race. And he went on to triumph in more Games, winning the long jump in a record four Olympics.

Carl Lewis

Ben Johnson

CHAPTER 10
Dreams Lost and Found:
The 1990s

In the 1990s, the Soviet Union broke up into Russia and many smaller countries. East and West Germany reunited. And a great change happened in South Africa.

The country had lived under apartheid, a system where people of color didn't have any of the same rights as whites. Everything was separated, including sports. South Africa wouldn't let blacks compete alongside whites. Because of this, the country had been banned from the Games. But apartheid finally ended. In 1992, in Barcelona, Spain, a South African team competed for the first time in thirty-six years.

AFRICA

SOUTH AFRICA

The women's 10,000-meter race (a little over five miles) featured two African runners. Elana Meyer was white and from South Africa. Derartu Tulu was black, and from Ethiopia. The two women led the pack. Finally, Tulu pulled ahead to finish first. She was the first black African woman to win a gold medal.

Meyer hugged her. Then Tulu grabbed Meyer's hand. Together, they started the victory lap. It was a historic image that captured the Olympic spirit.

Derartu Tulu and Elana Meyer

Other changes came to the Olympics. By 1992, pro athletes could compete in all sports. So for the first time, National Basketball Association superstars appeared at the Olympics. Some of the

most famous basketball players of all time teamed up. Michael Jordan. Magic Johnson. Larry Bird. Known as the Dream Team, it's sometimes called the greatest ever in any sport.

The closest game was the final—the United States against Croatia. The score: 117–85, with the United States taking gold. For the American players, it wasn't just about winning. Former NBA rivals now became close friends.

The medal ceremony, on the basketball court, was emotional. One player said it "sent chills down my spine."

But the games were most meaningful to Bird and Johnson. Those were the last games they played before retiring.

In 1996, one hundred years after the first modern Olympics, the United States hosted the Summer Games again, this time in Atlanta, Georgia.

Another Attack

On July 27, 1996, at 1:25 a.m., a bomb exploded in an Atlanta park. The park was not an official Olympic site, but it was crowded. Two people died and more than one hundred were injured. The bomber, an American terrorist, was finally arrested in 2003.

Often a host country feels an especially strong drive to win Olympic medals. This certainly was true in 1996. American women gymnasts were determined to be the first US gymnastics team to win gold.

In 1992, the team had taken bronze. Kerri Strug had competed then, and she was back. She'd never been a superstar. She stayed in the background. But this year, the team was depending on Strug's vault performance in the final event. If she nailed it, the United States would stay ahead of Russia and Romania.

Strug stood straight. She raised her arms over her head, signaling her start. Then she ran down the runway. She vaulted with a one and half twist. It looked good. But Strug fell on landing, injuring her ankle. Her score: a low 9.162.

Strug could barely stand. Still, she had one more try, and she wanted to take it. Blocking the pain, she raced down the runway. She jumped,

Kerri Strug

and stuck the landing. That meant she ended with a nearly perfect pose, barely moving her feet on touching the ground.

Only then, when Strug collapsed, did most people see her pain.

Her new score: 9.712.

The US team won! Strug was carried to the medal podium, already wearing a cast for her sprained ankle. She became a national hero. And the team became known as the Magnificent Seven.

CHAPTER 11
A New Century:
The 2000s

Australia hosted the 2000 Summer Olympics. Athletes gathered in Sydney for the "Millennium Games," the start of a new era.

During the opening ceremony, Australian runner Cathy Freeman lit the Olympic cauldron. Freeman had won silver in 1996. She was the first Aborigine to take part in an opening ceremony this way.

The Aborigine people have lived in Australia for thousands of years, long before Europeans arrived.

Cathy Freeman

As with African Americans, they'd been treated as second-class citizens.

Freeman was a symbol of Australian unity, and the whole country rooted for her. With more than a hundred thousand fans cheering, the pressure on her to win the 400-meter race was intense. But Freeman explained later that she was able to take in the audience's emotion and turn it into strength. She came out of third place and crossed the finish line first!

"What a legend!" one commentator said.

Overwhelmed, Freeman sat on the ground for a moment. When she took her victory lap, she held two flags: the Australian and the Aborigine.

Rulon Gardner

Unlike Freeman, no one expected much from US wrestler Rulon Gardner.

Gardner grew up on a dairy farm in Wyoming. He was big and tall. By the time he joined his high-school team, he was so big, kids called him "Fatso." Still, he was a standout athlete. And Gardner didn't let the name-calling get to him. He kept wrestling. And he made the Olympic team in Greco-Roman wrestling. But he'd never won a big competition. At Sydney he faced a three-time Greco-Roman Olympic champion.

Wrestling vs. Boxing

Wrestling and boxing are both "combat sports," a test of fighting skills between two athletes. Boxers hit opponents with their fists, trying to gain points by striking their opponents or to knock their opponents out. Wrestlers use clinches and throws to pin opponents to the mat. In freestyle, wrestlers use any part of their body to fight. In Greco-Roman, they only use their arms and upper body.

BOXING

WRESTLING

People called Russian Aleksandr Karelin "the Wrestler of the Century," "the Machine," and "the Russian Bear."

But twenty-nine-year-old Gardner was ready for the match. In the first period, Gardner dodged Karelin as best he could. The score at the end: 0–0.

In the second period, the wrestlers went into a clinch. But Gardner broke Karelin's grip. That gave him a point. Now Gardner knew he could win. He kept pushing at Karelin, not giving up his edge.

Gardner won, 1–0, and shocked the world. He shocked everyone even more by doing a perfect cartwheel to celebrate!

In 2004, the Summer Olympics came home to Athens, Greece. American swimmer Michael Phelps was nineteen. "The Baltimore Bullet" was born in Maryland, one of three children. When Phelps was little, he didn't like to put his face in the water. So he learned the backstroke first.

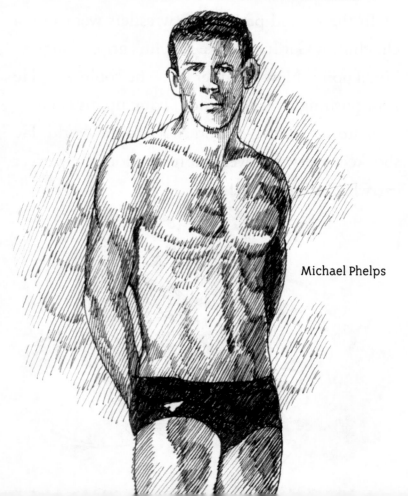

Michael Phelps

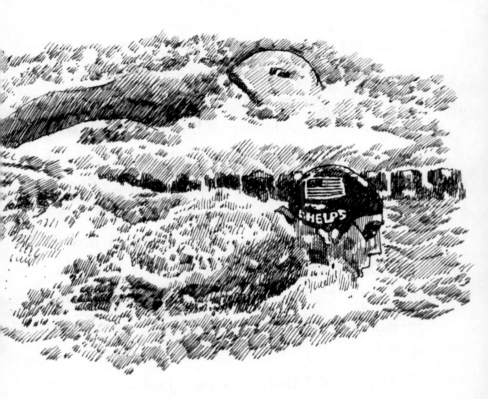

Phelps left Athens with six gold medals and two bronze. It was an amazing performance, but he hadn't beaten Mark Spitz's record—at least not yet. In Beijing, four years later, he was ready to win more gold.

In the 200-meter butterfly (four pool lengths), Phelps dove into the pool. For the stroke, he moved his arms together—up and out of the water, then forward and down—while he kicked both legs together. But something was wrong. His goggles were filling with water. His vision got worse and worse. But he didn't stop. Toward the end, he couldn't see a thing. When his fingers touched the wall, he had no idea he'd won!

Michael Phelps earned enough gold medals that Olympics to break Spitz's record. And after the 2012 Games, Phelps became one of the greatest Olympians of all time, with twenty-two medals.

At the 2008 Beijing Games, Jamaican runner Usain Bolt dashed into Olympic history. He set a world record in the 100-meter, took gold in the 200, and helped the Jamaican relay team to a championship.

But four years later, in London, it seemed his teammate Yohan Blake might overtake the "Lightning Bolt."

Once Bolt's feet hit the track, though, he left everyone far behind. "Yohan gave me a wake-up call," Bolt joked later. "He knocked on my door, and said, 'Usain, wake up! This is an Olympic year!'"

Bolt wound up winning three gold medals. And in 2016, he won three more. At the Olympic stadium in Rio de Janeiro, Brazil, fans packed the stands, rising to their feet to "Bolt." Copying the runner's special move after a win, they leaned back and pointed to the sky.

Rio would be Usain Bolt's last Olympics. And at the next Games? The stands would be empty.

CHAPTER 12
The Covid Olympics

In 2020, the outbreak of a dangerous new disease called COVID-19 shut down much of the world. The Tokyo Olympics were postponed. Instead, the Games were held in 2021. To help prevent any virus spread, spectators weren't allowed. Events were eerily quiet.

It was an Olympics like no other.

In gymnastics, Simone Biles went into the Games with a record nineteen world championship gold medals and four Olympic gold medals. The superstar felt enormous pressure. It was all too much.

In order to support her

mental health, Biles dropped out of the team event (the US still won silver), then the all-around (with teammate Sunisa "Suni" Lee taking gold). But courageously, Biles came back for one last event: the balance beam. She earned bronze, a prize that meant more, she said, than all her golds.

Two high jumpers made history. The friends— one from Qatar, the other from Italy—were in a tie for first place. Instead of competing in a "jump- off," they decided to share the title, breaking down in tears, then placing the gold medals around each other's necks.

These Games were about equality, too. At least 182 athletes proudly identified as part of the LGBTQ+ community. Women's soccer teams knelt to protest against racial injustice. Individual athletes did, too.

The Olympics will always remain a world stage for top athletes. Even in troubled times, its flame will always burn brightly.

Timeline of the Summer Olympics

c. 700s BC	Ancient Olympics begin in Olympia, Greece
c. AD 400s	Ancient Olympics come to an end
1896	First modern Olympics take place in Athens, Greece
1904	United States hosts for the first time in St. Louis, Missouri
1928	Women first compete in gymnastics and track and field
1948	Olympics resume after World War II
1956	Athletes from different countries march together at closing ceremonies for the first time
1960	Olympics are broadcast on television around the world for the first time
1968	Black American athletes protest for equality at Mexico City Games
1972	Eleven Israeli Olympians and a German police officer are killed in a terrorist attack during the Games in Munich, Germany
1980	United States boycotts the Moscow Games
1984	Soviet Union and allies boycott the Los Angeles Games
1992	After ending apartheid, South Africa competes for the first time since 1960
1996	Bomb explodes in Centennial Olympic Park in Atlanta, Georgia
2012	Jamaican sprinter Usain Bolt is acknowledged as the fastest man on earth, winning the 100-meter and 200-meter
2020	Due to the COVID-19 pandemic, the thirty-second Olympics are postponed until 2021

Timeline of the World

c. 700s BC	City-state of Athens gains power
AD 400s	Rise of Attila the Hun, warrior-king who attacked the Roman Empire
1896	Utah is admitted to the United States as the forty-fifth state
1904	US engineers begin work on the Panama Canal
1912	The "unsinkable" *Titanic* strikes an iceberg and sinks into the North Atlantic on April 15
1928	Sliced bread is sold for first time
1948	US president Truman ends racial segregation in the military
1956	Soviet Union invades Hungary
1968	Civil rights leader Martin Luther King Jr. is assassinated
1972	Apollo 17, the last manned mission to the moon, launches
1980	United States beats the Soviet Union during the Winter Olympics hockey tournament for a "Miracle on Ice"
1984	Democrat Geraldine Ferraro runs for US vice president but is not elected
1992	Cartoon Network premieres
1996	South Africa adopts a new constitution after apartheid ends
2012	Lonesome George, the last Pinta Island tortoise, dies
2020	NBA superstar Kobe Bryant dies in a helicopter crash along with one of his daughters and other passengers

Bibliography

*Books for young readers

Brown, Daniel James. *The Boys in the Boat: Nine Americans and Their Epic Quest for Gold at the 1936 Berlin Olympics*. New York: Viking, 2013.

Miller, David. *The Official History of the Olympic Games and the IOC: Athens to London, 1894–2012*. Edinburgh: Mainstream Publishing, 2012.

*Peters, Stephanie, and Matt Christopher. *The Olympics: Unforgettable Moments of the Games*. Legendary Sports Events. New York: Little, Brown and Company, 2008.

Tibballs, Geoff. *The Olympics' Strangest Moments: Extraordinary But True Tales from the History of the Olympic Games*. London: Robson Books, 2004.

Wallechinsky, David, and Jaime Loucky. *The Complete Book of the Olympics, 2012 Edition*. London: Aurum Press, 2012.